THE MISSION INDIANS
OF CALIFORNIA

MISSION INDIANS
OF CALIFORNIA

CHUMASH
DIEGUEÑO
SERRANO
GABRIELINO
JUANEÑO
LUISEÑO
CAHUILLA

CALIFORNIA

PACIFIC OCEAN

San Rafael Arcangel
SAN FRANCISCO
OAKLAND
San Francisco de Asís
Santa Clara de Asís
San José de Guadalupe

Santa Cruz
San Juan Bautista

MONTEREY
CARMEL • San Carlos Borromeo
Nuestra Señora de la Soledad

San Antonio de Padua
• San Miguel Arcangel

San Luis Obispo de Tolosa
La Purísima

Santa Ines
Santa Barbara
SANTA BARBARA
San Buenaventura
San Fernando Rey
San Gabriel Arcangel
LOS ANGELES

San Juan Capistrano
San Luis Rey

SAN DIEGO
San Diego de Alcala

The
MISSION
INDIANS
OF CALIFORNIA

By SONIA BLEEKER

Illustrated by Althea Karr

WILLIAM MORROW & COMPANY
New York • 1956

For my husband, Herbert S. Zim.

Copyright 1956 by Sonia Bleeker. Printed in the United States of America. All rights reserved. Published simultaneously in the Dominion of Canada by George J. McLeod Limited, Toronto. Library of Congress Catalog Card Number: 56-5867.

CONTENTS

Chapter

Grateful recognition is given to
Dr. Edward W. Gifford,
Museum of Anthropology, University of California,
Berkeley, California,
for reading and criticizing the manuscript.

I

LITTLE SINGER'S FIRST CEREMONY

Ever since he could remember, everyone in the village had called him Little Singer. Even now, when he was old enough for the boys' initiation ceremony, they still did. "Sit here, Little Singer," a man or woman would invite him, when the people came together. "Sit with us."

9

Like the other boys in his small village by the creek, in what is now southern California, Little Singer did not often think of his real name. This name, chosen by his grandparents, had belonged to a dead relative whose spirit now shone as a star in the sky. It had been given him, soon after his birth, at a birthday feast in the village big house—

the ceremonial house—where all his father's relatives had gathered. On that occasion the village chief had picked him up and, holding him for everyone to see, had spoken his chosen name. But it was against custom for anyone to repeat it.

These Indians believed that a name had particular power. Some of the power of the man or woman to whom it had belonged in the past remained with it. The baby who received this name inherited with it some of the power of its former owner. A successful hunter's name was believed to have the power needed for good hunting. The name of a woman who was especially good at making acorn bread held some of that particular power. The people believed that a girl given this name would make a good housewife and that a boy who received a famed hunter's name would surely turn into a good hunter.

The people also believed that their medicine men, or shamans (shay-muns), could take away some of a person's power if they knew his real name. The shamans knew special songs and dances that had an effect upon people. By singing these songs and performing these dances, the shamans won the attention of the spirits and made them do their bidding. But a spirit, so the people believed, had to know the name of the victim in order to work him harm. So no one in a village willingly told the names of his family or neighbors to outsiders, for fear evil might come to them. Even though most of the people in a village were related, and wished each other no harm, everyone felt it was safer to be called by a nickname. Everyone also liked to be called Brother or Sister, Father or Mother, Uncle, Grandfather, or Grandmother, not only by his own family, but by others in the village as well. For these names were spoken with affection and respect.

Little Singer had earned his nickname when he was only a few years old. At that time, Father was invited to a neighboring village where some of his relatives lived. He was to help at a girls' initiation ceremony. Mother went with Father, to help him, and they took Sister and Little Singer along, too. To the boy, the neighboring village looked just like his own. Spreading live oaks grew everywhere. Willows and cottonwoods shaded the banks of the river. About a dozen small huts, covered with mats and grass thatching, nestled in the shade of the live oaks. In the center of the village was a larger house, also covered with thatching, where the chief lived and the village ceremonies and dances were held.

The preparations for the girls' ceremony had already begun. Four girls in the village were now old enough, at the age of thirteen or fourteen, to enter womanhood. This initiation ceremony marked the step into womanhood, and they were all happy to have reached this stage. Such initiation ceremonies were held once or twice a year in each village. These ceremonies had to be performed with the greatest care, since it was believed that a girl's entire future depended on them. Her health and happiness, her marriage, the bearing of children, and the health of her husband and children hung upon the strict observance of each ceremonial detail.

According to custom, a chief had to perform this ceremony. He must come from another village, but he must be of a related clan. The girls' parents had worked hard hunting and gathering food for the feast. They had accumulated enough provisions in the village chief's large storage baskets to feed the visiting chief and the other guests who always came for ceremonies, and to make them gifts of food.

The mothers of the girls helped clean up and sweep the hut outside the village where the girls were to stay, and covered it with brush. The fathers helped dig the large pit where the four girls were to rest during the ceremony. The mothers built fires in the pit and heated large flat stones in them. They swept the pit clean, spread sand and branches on its floor, put in the heated stones, and covered them with brush.

Each of the girls brought with her a small

bundle of the things she would need: her hair-brush, made of fine twigs or pounded yucca fibers, and some grated yucca root for soap; her wooden bowl and spoon; her necklace, earrings, arm bands, and a scratcher made of abalone shell. If a girl touched her body or face with her hands during this ceremonial time, it was thought that she would get pimples. Every girl wanted a smooth skin, so she was careful to follow the custom and use her abalone scratcher.

Little Singer's father started the ceremony by giving the girls a small ball of tobacco leaves to swallow. Women did not smoke tobacco. Most men smoked only during ceremonies. Only old men smoked at home. Everyone believed that smoke pleased the spirits. After swallowing the tobacco, each of the girls lay down in the pit on the warm sand and stones. Their mothers put warm stones on their stomachs and covered them with rushes and mats. The girls had to lie in the pit for three days. During the day the girls' mothers stayed near them, talking to them, fanning them, and keeping the stones warm. The girls ate very little at this time, only some acorn mush in the morning. No meat, fish, or salt was permitted. At night, men and women gathered near the pit to dance. Men who knew songs about the moon were invited by the girls' parents to come and sing for their daughters and for the dancers. The moon, they believed, was also a woman, and women's special friend. The moon watched over them and had taught them about these ceremonies long ago when she lived on earth.

While Mother was busy helping Father, she seated the boy next to one of the singers. The boy listened to the singer, although the song was strange to him. He could not understand a word of it, for it was in a language he had never heard before. This was not unusual among these southern California Indians, who had different languages and spoke them in various dialects, or local ways of speaking. A song was considered sacred, no matter what language it was sung in. Some of the songs were so old that the people did not know the language to which they had originally belonged.

As the singer, shaking his turtle-shell rattle, repeated the song a few times, the boy began to move his hand in rhythm, whispering the strange words. He had seen older boys learning songs in this way. As the singer started the song anew, the boy raised his voice and sang the song with him. The singer was surprised and pleased. Songs were valued, but a singer was glad to teach his songs to the boys of the tribe. People brought their children to ceremonies so they would have a chance to learn songs. It took some youngsters many days to master a song completely, but this boy sang the song perfectly after hearing it only three times.

The singer handed his rattle to the boy and told him to sing the song again while he got some water from a tall basket jar in the shade. Holding the turtle-shell rattle the way the singer had, the boy raised his voice and sang.

Ki-ima, ki-ima
Pok nyawiyu
Myu-wiw-kaya
Ki-ima, ki-ima

Everyone stopped dancing and turned to look at the little singer. The boy was shy at first, but he had to keep on singing. A song once started must be finished. He sang the song twice before he handed the turtle-shell rattle back to its owner. The singer was glad to get this extra attention for his song. "Little Singer, we shall sing together," he said.

The singer started another song. This time the words were in the boy's own language. After listening to the simple song twice, the boy was sure he knew it, so he sang it. By the time Mother came for him, the boy knew several songs. The tired dancers, cheered by his small, fresh voice, put more vigor into their simple heel-and-toe steps around the fire.

Next day, to test Little Singer's memory, Father asked him to sing the songs he had learned the night before. He gave Little Singer a small gourd rattle and the boy, accompanying himself, sang the songs perfectly. The following evening, while the other singers were resting, Little Singer sang for the girls. A girl's mother brought him freshly baked acorn bread and her father presented him with a turtle-shell rattle. Their daughter liked his singing very much.

The chief of a neighboring village, who had also come for the ceremony, spoke to Little Singer's father. Their village planned a mourning ceremony several moons later, and they wanted Little Singer to help them. Everyone was sure that Little Singer's sweet voice would please the spirits of the dead, whom they were honoring with this mourning ceremony and feast. During the girls' ceremony, Little Singer sat next to several singers and learned many songs.

After lying for three days in the warm sand, the girls got up and bathed in the creek. Little Singer's mother painted their faces with red and black lines, and the girls put on fresh knee-length skirts made of pounded and woven cedar bark and yucca fiber. Next they put on shell necklaces and arm and ankle bands made of twisted hair. Their own mothers combed their long hair. The girls were allowed to walk about the village now, but for another month or two they still had to watch their food. They were allowed to eat very little and to drink only warm water.

During the month that little Singer and his family spent in this village, he and the other boys of his age played the same games he had played in his own village and ran races every day. This exercise would strengthen their legs, so when they grew older they would not mind the long hunting trips that men had to undertake. They also practiced shooting birds with their bows and blunt arrows. There were birds everywhere, large and small. Their meat added very little to the cooking pot, but their colorful feathers were welcome as ornaments. The boys set out snares for rabbits and gophers, and played shinny, their favorite game. They played it on a field near the village, using a stick like our field-hockey or ice-hockey stick and a ball stuffed with grass. The boys formed two teams, each with its own goal at opposite ends of the field.

When the girls' initiation ceremony reached its final stage at the end of the month, everyone came to the ceremonial house. The men had gathered sand of several colors. Little Singer's father, together with several helpers, spread sand all over the floor in the ceremonial house. Then, with black sand, they outlined a large circle which represented the earth and the sky. Within this circle they drew pictures, with sand of different

colors. The things they drew were important in their religious beliefs: a snake, the Milky Way, different medicinal plants, the sun, the moon, and clouds. The snake was important because he guarded the house of the creator of the earth and sky. The Milky Way was the trail that led the spirits of the dead to their new home in the sky.

One of the girls stepped up to the sand painting and knelt before it. The chief touched her head,

shoulders, arms, and chest with a pellet of sage meal mixed with salt and then put the pellet into her mouth. The girl spat the pellet into the center of the sand painting, where a small hole had been dug to receive it. The chief now spoke to the girl, telling her to be good and kind, to work hard, and to be generous with the food she gathered and cooked. He told her to heed the advice of the old people and to take care of them. This ceremony was repeated for each girl. When it was over, the girls lined up in the fields behind the village and ran a race.

After the chief's words, the helpers had scooped up the entire sand painting carefully and taken the sand out of the village. They poured it under a rock, so no one would step on this sacred sand.

Now Little Singer's mother painted the girls' faces again. Some of the mothers asked her to tattoo their daughters' faces. With a thorn, Mother pricked lines on the girls' chins, upper lips, and cheeks, and rubbed charcoal mixed with fat into the tiny holes. Tattooing, like very long hair, was thought very becoming for a woman.

Little Singer and his family had barely returned to his village when a messenger from another village came to invite them to a ceremony. He especially wanted Little Singer to come, for the people of his village had heard how well the boy had sung at the girls' initiation ceremony. So Mother got her large pack basket ready. She

asked the messenger to wait until she made a few
extra pairs of sandals for the family.

Two days before, Mother had buried in the

sand by the creek some pounded, fibrous leaves
of yucca that she had picked in the dry places near
their village. Now she took the fibers out of the

sand and combed them. She twisted them into thick coils as long as a person's foot and sewed them together, using some more twisted fiber for thread. Her awl was a piece of bone that had been ground on a rock to give it a sharp point. She made a loop of the twisted thread at the back of the sandal to hold the wearer's heel, and fastened two long strings to the front of the sandal. These would be passed around the wearer's second toe and tied over the instep.

When the sandals were finished, the family hung a mat over the opening of their hut, to show that no one was at home. Now they were ready to follow the messenger up the narrow trails to his village.

"The women are planning to move our village," Mother told the messenger. "There are more plants up the creek. Here we have picked all the plants and the houses are getting shabby and wind-worn."

In those days, less than two centuries ago, hundreds of Indian villages dotted the foothills, valleys, and seacoast of southern California. This warm region, with its dry, hot summers and mild, rainy winters was a pleasant place to live. It is believed that there were over 30,000 Indians in southern California at that time, in the region south of the Tehachapi Mountains. These people did no farming. The men hunted and snared small game. The men of the villages along the Pacific coast and near rivers fished the year round. However, the women of the entire region did most of the food getting. They gathered acorns from the live oaks that covered their country. They also gathered pine and other nuts and grass seed, edible roots, bulbs, and flowers.

The people did not have to worry much about clothing. The men and boys wore no clothes and usually went barefoot. For long trips the women made sandals. In cool weather a buckskin or rabbitskin blanket was thrown over the shoulders.

The women wore short skirts that looked like double aprons. They were made of yucca or bark fibers.

Men and women, boys and girls, all wore ornaments: shell necklaces, earrings, arm and ankle bands. Both men and women had their faces tattooed and wore their hair long. An important daily task for a woman was to comb her husband's and children's long hair with a yucca brush.

After the winter rains, or whenever the houses in a village became weather-beaten and the nearby plants used up, the people packed their belongings and moved up or down the creek to build another village. As the years passed, each group began to look upon certain tracts of land as its own territory. No other group was allowed to move a village into this territory unless it had special permission from the village chiefs. If the group moved without this permission, it brought on a war. Although these southern Californians were for the most part a peaceful people, none of them hesitated to go to battle, raid an enemy, burn his village, and scalp anyone who was not quick enough to get away. In turn, the relatives of the people who were killed looked for revenge. So inter-village feuds flared up from time to time, followed by long periods of peace.

Most of the early names of these original Indian groups have been forgotten. The names by which we know them now, and the territory they inhabited, are shown on the map. These were names given them by their Spanish conquerors, late in the eighteenth century. They are pronounced as shown below:

Chumash (choo'-mahsh) Indians

Serrano (seh-rrah'-naw)—meaning those of the Sierras

Gabrielino (gab-ree-ay-lee'-naw)—because they lived in and around the mission of San Gabriel

Luiseño (loo-ee-zay'-nyaw)—living in and around the mission of San Luis Rey de Francia

Diegueño (dee-ay-gay′-nyaw)—living in and
around the mission of San Diego de Alcala

Juaneño (hwan-nay′-nyaw)—living in and
around the mission of San Juan Capistrano

Cahuilla (kah-wee′-ya). Although the spelling
is Spanish, the name is not. It is what these
Indian groups called themselves. Because they
lived inland, they had very little to do with
the missions—all of which were built on the
Pacific coast.

2

ACORN BREAD

The food the California Indians used came from many places. From early childhood everyone began to learn to gather food. There were not many times during the year when a home was entirely without food. But it did not come in the abundant harvests we are accustomed to getting from our big stretches of cornfields, wheat fields, orchards, and truck gardens. Unlike other Indian tribes, the southern California Indians grew none of the food they ate. To get food the men and boys hunted, snared game, and fished. The women gathered edible seeds and roots.

The most nourishing food was made from acorns. No one knows just when the southern California Indians learned to make use of the quantities of acorns in their oak forests. This achievement was as remarkable as the development of corn from wild grasses in early Central America. Since acorns contain tannin, which is a poison, the Indians had to learn to get rid of it before acorns could be used as a food. They had done this long ago, by leaching, or washing, the acorn flour, which made it safe to eat.

Making acorn bread took a long time. First, of course, the acorns had to be gathered. The

California live oaks, or encinas, as the Spanish later called them, grow some fifty feet high, with broad, dense crowns. Their heavy branches spread out horizontally and irregularly, making them excellent shade trees. In most of these oaks the leaves are stiff and leathery. There are several kinds of live oaks, and their common names tell the places where they thrive. They are the coast live oak, the interior live oak, the mesa oak, and the canyon oak. All of them bear acorns.

Acorns ripen in the fall. At that time families moved to places where they had always gathered acorns. Each family or group of relatives moved into the same shelter year after year. They regarded these acorn grounds as their territory, on which no one must trespass. If anyone did so unintentionally, he might be allowed to leave unharmed. But if the trespassing was intentional, the trespasser might be killed, for these Indians valued their acorn territory highly.

Acorns were stored in huge covered baskets,

which the women made. Some of these baskets were so large that children could play inside of them. Each family tried to stretch its supply of acorns from one harvest to the next.

Women ground acorns into flour almost daily. Little Singer's mother and sister were usually up at dawn on the day they planned to bake acorn bread. Mother had put the acorns to soak in a large olla (ohl'-ya), or basket jar, the day before. She now took them out of the water and shelled them.

Several stone mortars and flat grinding stones, or, as the Spanish later called them, metates (meh-tah'-tays), were lined up outdoors in the shade. Mother put a handful of the shelled acorns into a mortar, and Sister ground them with a stone pestle. Mother kept sifting the meal made by grinding the acorns, separating the finely ground meal from the coarse. She threw the very coarse meal back into the mortar and ground the finer meal on her metate. In this way, handful after handful, the acorn nuts were reduced to flour.

With a basketful of freshly ground flour, Mother and Sister went to the creek to leach the poisonous tannin from the flour. Mother's experience had taught her that flour which had been leached about ten times made the best-tasting bread. Accordingly, she took with her a bundle of ten sticks, to keep count.

Other women were also on their way to the creek. They, too, had been up since dawn, grinding acorns into flour. Now, loaded with baskets and bundles, they came trooping down to the creek. Several of the women carried babies. Since they planned to be away for many hours, the babies would have to be nursed. An older child of three or four could be left with a grandmother or older sister, but a baby had to be carried in its narrow cradleboard wherever its mother went. The mother bore the cradleboard on her back, fastened to a fiber strap slung over her forehead, and carried her basket of acorn flour on her head. A child of two might be carried in a big burden basket on Mother's or Older Sister's back.

Each woman laid her little bundle of sticks near the place where she always leached her acorn flour. She placed her baskets and trays in their customary places and then knelt down near some small holes to leach the flour. The women who had arrived earlier had already built fires and were boiling water in clay pots. While the water was heating, each poured her flour into one or more leaching holes. These were shallow, sandy holes. For the first leaching, Mother poured cold water over the flour. As the water slowly seeped through the flour in the hole, it washed out some of the tannin. The water over the fire was hot by the time she was ready for the second leaching. To keep count of the number of times she washed her flour, Mother laid aside a stick from her bundle each time she completed one washing.

While the water was seeping through the flour,

Mother and Sister went down to the creek to bathe. They removed their apronlike skirts and stepped in. The warm and shallow water was not very refreshing. Mother looked at the grass, brown from lack of rain. The weather will remain dry and dusty, she thought, until we have finished gathering acorns. Then the rains will come and the creek will fill with cold water from the mountains. The grass and shrubs will turn green almost overnight, and the flowers will burst into bloom. Mother thought of this with pleasure. Everything will be free of dust for a while. The hot winds will stop. It will be more comfortable to work outdoors.

But the rains always brought dampness, too. No matter how well the people plastered the chinks in their houses with mud and thatching, rain managed to seep in. Baskets and mats got moldy quickly. Children and old people often came down with the coughing sickness. But as soon as the rains stopped, discomfort and sickness were forgotten. The houses and mats were soon dry, and all was well again. Everyone hastened to gather flower petals to be dried and ground, and grass seed to be ground into meal.

The women ground up everything edible. They even ground rabbit bones and the hollow bones of birds shot down by the children, and mixed the bone meal with acorn flour when making bread.

Other women had also wandered off from the leaching holes. Some were gathering the willow shoots and rushes that grew by the creek for making baskets, since every household needed many baskets. Some women were making coiled basket trays from the little bundles of rushes and yucca fiber they had brought with them. Coiling a basket was like sewing. A woman first bent a frame of twisted grass or willow twigs into the shape of the basket or tray she planned to make. Next, with a sharpened chip of bone or thorn for an awl, she made tiny holes in the grass core of the tray and, with Indian hemp yarn, sewed the spiral foundation, row upon row, till the tray was finished. Some of the fibers had been dyed deep black in mud, some red and brown with plant dyes; still others had been bleached white in the sand. Each woman worked the different colors into the spiral foundation in a pleasing design.

While waiting for the third leaching to seep through the holes, Mother took a bundle of Indian hemp stalks she had gathered and placed the stalks on a flat rock. She pounded them with another flat stone till the fibers began to separate.

Now Mother pulled the Indian hemp fibers out of the pounded mass, one by one, and began to twist them together, two at a time, to make a strong yarn. She rolled the yarn on her thigh to help twist the fibers. Sister wound the yarn as Mother finished twisting it.

It was long past midday when Sister poured the last potful of hot water over the acorn flour and Mother picked up the last stick from her bundle. She tied the bundle of sticks with a piece of hemp yarn and loaded everything into a burden basket. Sister carried the basket on her back, as usual, while Mother carried the small basketful of acorn flour home.

When they reached home, Father had already returned from his hunting. Little Singer helped him skin the rabbits he had caught. The women-folk started a fire, with Little Singer's help. He twirled a pointed stick in a grooved board laid over dry grass. The heat from the twirling stick made the grass smoke. Sister blew on the smoking grass till it sparked, and Mother's fire was lighted. Over it, on supporting stones, she placed a clay pot with water in it. When the water came to a boil, she poured some of the acorn flour into it and kept stirring it with a stick till the mixture began to simmer. The pinkish flour soon turned into a thick mush that smelled like cocoa. Mother added neither salt nor any other flavoring to the mush. Sister and Little Singer placed flat stones to heat in the fire, on which to broil the rabbit meat. When the meal was ready, they scooped up the acorn mush from the serving tray with their fingers and carefully saved the rabbit bones to be ground and mixed with acorn flour for the next meal.

Evening was a time for people to get together.

Neighbors visited each other, exchanging news and gossip. People talked about coming ceremonies. Parents and grandparents told stories to their children. After tonight's meal, a neighbor dropped in to tell Father about his hunt that day.

Game was never abundant, and these Indians restricted themselves even further by refraining from eating certain animals. Most groups did not eat dogs, for example, although some did. No one ate coyotes or birds of prey, such as ravens, vultures, or eagles. They snared eagles, of course, for their valued feathers, but they did not eat the meat. Although the people ate all kinds of fish, including shellfish, they did not eat frogs or turtles. Because the ancestors of some of these animals played important roles in their legends, custom forbade eating them. The frog, for example, was supposed to be a daughter of Wiyot, their legendary hero.

Once, so goes the legend, Wiyot looked at

Frog and told her she was very ugly. This offended Frog. She had very powerful medicine and used it to make her father, Wiyot, very ill. Because he had taught the people everything they knew, the people did not want Wiyot to die. They carried him far away from his daughter, but her evil medicine reached Wiyot no matter where the people hid him. During his long illness Wiyot sang songs constantly, and this kept him from dying. The people listened to his songs and learned many of them. To this day, these songs are sung to cure ailments. As time went on, however, and Frog continued using her evil medicine, Wiyot grew weaker and weaker, and finally died. The people burned his body, as Wiyot told them to do; but Coyote, the trickster, stole Wiyot's heart and ran away with it. Wiyot went up to the sky and turned into the moon.

So the people did not eat the meat of the coyote, because they might have been eating Wiyot's heart.

For this same reason, the people did not eat bear meat. Bears look so human that the people suspected certain powerful shamans (medicine men) had turned themselves into bears purposely, hoping people would kill them and eat them. Then they would be cannibals, and no southern California Indian wanted to become a cannibal.

This evening the neighbor told Little Singer's father that he had seen a bear in the woods. Of

course he did not shoot him. He said the bear had
seen him and followed him. One never knew
whether the animal was really a bear or a shaman
in disguise. Frightened because he was all alone,
the neighbor began to run. He was a good runner
and soon left the large, lumbering animal behind.
It could be that some shaman was prowling about
as a bear, trying to harm someone in the village.

Father, the neighbor, and Little Singer went to

the village chief's house to talk things over. The village chief agreed that the bear should be killed. If he was a shaman, it would be right to kill him and stop his evil doings. They had killed shamans in the past because they suspected they were doing evil and bringing sickness to the village.

These Indians believed that sickness was an evil thing that entered a person's body only through the evil medicine of another person, a shaman, or a spirit. And sickness had to be sucked out of the body, as one sucks out the poison from a snake bite. Medicine men, or shamans, knew how to do this.

When a person felt ill, his family called in a medicine man to cure him. First, the shaman asked the patient where the sickness hurt him most. Next, the shaman sang some special songs that he knew; then he put his mouth to the part of the body that hurt, and sucked it. He usually showed the family a pebble or some other small object that he had sucked out, and promised them that their relative would get well. If the patient did not get well, the shaman sang still more songs and sucked the patient's body again. A family spared no effort in getting the right shaman to cure a patient. When one failed, they in-

vited another and gave each one many gifts for his work. They believed that a person died only because the sickness was too strong for the power their shamans had.

Several hunters went out the following day and killed the bear. They examined the carcass, but could not tell whether it had been a shaman or a real bear. They left the carcass in the woods for the eagle, the vulture, and the raven to feast upon.

3

THE NEW MOON

Little Singer's remarkable memory made him
a favorite among the southern California Indians.
By the time he was twelve years old, invitations
for him and his parents were coming from many
villages, some as far away as three days' walk.
Some of the invitations were not even from rel-

atives (people whose clan name was the same as his father's). The people had heard of Little Singer and wanted him to help them out—to make their ceremony better and more pleasing to the spirits. Little Singer was no longer as excited as he had been at first. A messenger usually came to their hut with small gifts for his parents: a carefully woven basket for his mother or a small pouch of tobacco for his father. Once or twice a messenger from a distant village brought an especially welcome gift—a small string of shells. These shells, collected on the islands near the California mainland and traded inland, were valued as highly by the California Indians as we value money.

One day, while Little Singer was playing with his friends in the field outside their village, they saw two messengers entering their village. They looked very important. Their faces were heavily painted, and the older man wore many necklaces. The boys stopped playing, followed the messengers, and saw them stop at the village chief's house. The chief then led them to Little Singer's house.

The messengers, a chief and his son, had come to invite Little Singer to their village for the boys' initiation ceremonies. They brought three strings of shells—for Little Singer, his father, and his mother. Their village was on the Pacific coast, four days' journey away.

It was hard to understand the language the strangers spoke. Many of the words were like the words in Little Singer's language, but the visiting chief had to repeat many others and explain them by pointing to the things they stood for. The strangers' language was related to Little Singer's, but these coastal tribes had been living away from his for so long, and their language had become so different, that everyone recognized it as a different dialect.

The chief's son, Kwamut, was older than Little Singer. He was about sixteen. Many boys of his age had already been initiated, but there had been no initiation ceremony in their village the year before. Now several boys of the right age—from thirteen to sixteen—were ready for initiation. That was why they considered the ceremony especially important and had come to invite Little Singer. Kwamut told the boys of the village about the Great Water where he went fishing almost every day. He had his own canoe, he said, and he gathered many shells. Little Singer found himself eager to go.

This time Mother decided to let Older Sister go, too. Sister was fifteen now, and ready to be married. Mother was anxious for her to learn how to care for a household, to make baskets and pottery, and gather the right plants to feed a family. It was hard for a girl to learn these things unless she could do them every day. So when the family traveled, Sister had usually lived with an aunt who had small children whom she could take care of, and she helped with household tasks.

The visiting chief and his son stayed in Little Singer's house, and the men from the rest of the village came in the evening to talk and smoke with the chief. They brought small gifts of rabbits or whatever meat they had killed that day. Since Father was busy with the visitors, he did not go hunting. The women brought Mother ground acorn flour. Sister and Mother cooked and served the guests. These Indians' hospitality customs called for serving food to visitors at any time of the day or night, so Sister and Mother kept busy by the fire, warming acorn mush or broiling meat. Little Singer and Kwamut went hunting together and shot a deer. This would have made a fine feast for them, but it was the first deer either of the boys had ever shot, and custom demanded that they give the meat to an old man— a neighbor.

That night, as the men sat talking and the women were busy by the fire, they could smell the venison steaks being broiled by the old man's daughter-in-law. Just as Mother brought in a wooden bowl full of acorn mush and placed it before the visitors, the daughter-in-law came in,

carrying a huge basket tray piled high with freshly broiled venison. The boys were very happy that everyone enjoyed the special treat.

Their mouths watered for a taste of the steaks, but they were not allowed to touch them. Only after a boy had grown to manhood was he allowed to eat the deer meat he himself had shot. If he ate it before that time, it might make him very sick and he might never again shoot a deer, so the people believed.

Usually the two boys liked to sit up late listening to the men talk, but tonight they lay down on their sleeping places soon after the evening meal. "There is going to be a race tomorrow night, because of the new moon, and we must rest," Little Singer told Kwamut, as he settled himself for the night.

According to the beliefs of some of these Indians, the wise and good man, Wiyot, hero of their legends, turned into the moon when he died. While he was living, Wiyot taught the people all they knew and even taught them many of their sacred songs. So they honored him monthly with a ceremony, when he reappeared in the sky as the new moon.

Other tribes of southern California believed that the new moon was once a beautiful woman, who lived with the people for a long time and taught the women and girls special things about child care. She taught them their lullabies and the songs they sang to help an ailing child get well. However, rather than marry her creator, Mukat, whom she did not love, Moon left the people and went up to the sky. It was to honor her return each month that the boys of these tribes raced on the first night of the new moon.

As the sun neared the horizon, it grew colder. The people threw rabbitskin blankets over their shoulders. While the villagers gathered in the field, talking and laughing, an old man lined up the boys for the race. At a sign from him, they began to run westward, toward the bright sliver of the new moon. They reached the foot of the hill

with Kwamut far ahead of the rest of the boys.
According to custom, Kwamut, after winning the
race, dashed across in front of the line of runners.
This finished the race.

All the parents were sure now that their sons
would grow rapidly as the moon grew bigger and
rounder each night. The moon would watch over

them to see them grow strong and remain well.

In the village, the women were hovering over their cooking fires. The boys joined their families by the fires. The smell of roasted rabbit meat and baked acorn bread made them even hungrier. Most of the boys had eaten nothing all day. They had purposely gone hungry so the spirits would feel sorry for them and help them win the race. The younger children were very fond of the sweetish, pink acorn bread. They preferred it to the charred rabbit meat.

"Come, Little Singer, sit here." The village chief motioned the boy to a seat next to him. Kwamut also sat at the village chief's side, in the seat of honor, because he had won the race.

Little Singer shook his turtle-shell rattle. In the silence that followed, his high-pitched, boyish voice could be heard to the far ends of the village. He sang the song to the moon, the first song he had learned during the girls' initiation ceremony. No one in the gathering, including Little

Singer, understood the strange language of the song. This did not trouble anyone, for the all-knowing moon would understand the song and in response bring good things to the people.

4

KWAMUT'S VILLAGE

Little Singer and his family left for the coastal village the morning after the new moon ceremony. They walked up the trail in single file— first the chief, then Father, Mother, Sister, Little Singer, and last of all Kwamut, the chief's son. Mother and Sister carried large baskets on their backs, placed in nets, and supported by woven straps that went around their foreheads. To keep the weight of their loads from pressing the straps too hard against the skin of their foreheads, Mother and Sister wore low-fitting caps that looked like baskets turned upside down. Father, the chief, and the two boys carried bows and arrows. Each had a rabbit stick tucked into his belt. The belts, made of twisted fiber, were worn for the journey.

The first day of the trip was very hot. After walking all morning along the narrow dusty trail, it was a relief to sit down at midday under an oak and rest till the sun's rays began to slant from the west. In the distance, on a hill, was a village that looked deserted. Little Singer could not recall ever having seen this village before. He was about to go with Kwamut to get a closer look at it, when he saw two boys come out of a house, carrying two large ollas filled with water. Little Singer knew now how glad strangers who came to his village must be when he gave them water. These boys had been left with the old people while the rest of the village had gone to gather food, and they were glad of the chance to speak to strangers. Kwamut gave each of them a shell, and the boys invited him and Little Singer to come up to the village, but the chief wanted to keep pushing ahead.

They slept that night in a shelter near the trail. In the morning Mother and Sister carefully cleaned up the shelter and left everything in order. This day was also uneventful. Again they rested at noon. Then they filled their gourds with water from a nearby spring and continued walking. The chief knew the road and the distances between villages. He planned each day's march so that they would reach that night's shelter in time to hunt for a few rabbits while the women made a fire. One day they met a party of three men going east for a ceremony and chatted with them for a while. The chief told them about the trails, and the men gave the travelers some of the meat they had left over from their noonday meal. They also gave Mother a rabbitskin.

At midday on the fourth day, Little Singer saw the Great Water (the Pacific Ocean) for the first time. He stood long in amazement and wonder, gazing at the vast stretch of turquoise-blue water. From the legends he had heard, he knew that this Great Water surrounded and held the entire earth. What a great mass of water without end, always moving, moving, wave upon wave, beating against the earth's ends! Because this was the time of the new moon, the tides were high. The sky above the water was blue and cloudless. Kwamut pushed Little Singer lightly, to urge him to go on. And Little Singer walked on, half stumbling, his eyes on the water till it disappeared from view in a wooded part of the trail.

When they reached the chief's village, his two wives welcomed Little Singer's family and made them comfortable inside their cool house. It was

a large, square structure with a sloping, thatched roof. The walls, also covered with thatch, were plastered with mud. The floor was about a foot below the outside level. It had been dug out and stamped down to make it level. Along the walls were sleeping platforms. The house was divided into four compartments. Two were occupied by the chief's wives. Little Singer's family moved into the third. The fourth and largest had a fire

pit, where the chief's family did their cooking in cool weather.

Kwamut picked up his fishing tackle and took Little Singer and Sister down to the Great Water. The water was warm and salty and—to Little Singer's surprise as he scooped it in his cupped hands—colorless. Yet the great expanse of it looked so blue!

Kwamut jumped into the water and swam

away. Little Singer hesitated; he had not learned to swim. Their creek back home had too little water in it during the summer. In the rainy season it was full, but the swift-flowing current was too cold for enjoyable swimming. So Little Singer and his sister wandered over to a spot where several boats and rafts were tied to posts and rocks. Never before had either of the children seen a boat or a raft.

Several rafts were turned over and beached to dry. These rafts, sometimes called balsas, were made of bundles of cattails and tule rushes that grew in the brackish water of inlets. Men, women, and children gathered these. When they had a big enough stack, the men tied the bundles together and made them into cigar-shaped rafts. These rafts were never completely waterproof. After being in the water for a while, they got soggy and had to be beached and dried.

The boats interested the children even more. There were only two of them, about three times as long as a man's height, and very narrow. They were made of boards lashed together and calked with tar. Since the Indians in those days did not have axes or saws they used wedges, made of stone or whalebone, to cut boards. The cedars from which the boards were made grew inland in the foothills. The men went to the woods with their families, camped there, and spent several days getting boards.

On the first day they set fire to the base of the tree they wanted to bring down. As the wood burned, they chipped away the charred part with their chisel-like wedges and stone hammers, and continued burning the tree till it toppled over. Then they hammered in wedges at the base till they split the tree trunk. The boards, of course, were not as smooth or thin as the boards we make today. After the men had enough long boards, they carried them down to a nearby river and floated them to the ocean.

Finally, when the boards had become thoroughly dry, the men began to shape them to make a boat. The edges of each board were perforated with stone-pointed drills so the boards could be lashed edge to edge.

Besides learning the use of wedges, the people had made another important discovery. They had learned to use tar to cement boards together and make their boats waterproof. We do not know just when these Indians discovered how to use tar. We now know that where oil deposits near the ground dry up, because of evaporation, a residue of bitumen, or tar, is left. This black, sticky residue forms in pools and lakes. The deposits at La Brea, California—west of Los Angeles—are now world-famous. In those days the Indians used this tar as we use glue.

Carrying his fishing tackle, Kwamut came and joined the two children. After picking up a double-bladed paddle and a long pole, he untied one of the balsas. Little Singer and Sister knelt in the center of it while he showed them how to

use the double paddle. Then he poled the balsa away from shore.

Neither of the two young inlanders had ever been out on the water before. Sister held on tight to the low sides of the balsa, while Little Singer gripped the double paddle and held it against the side.

Kwamut handed his pole to Sister. While Little Singer steadied the balsa with his paddle, Kwamut put some abalone bait on his fishhook and cast his line. The fishhook was made of the spiral of an abalone shell, and the fishline of twisted Indian hemp.

The Indians had found out that with each new moon the tides are very high and very low. At very low tide it was a good time to go out looking for abalone, oysters, clams, and other shellfish. At high tide it was a good time to go fishing.

The single-shelled abalone clings to rocks near the shore. The Indians knew this and they pried them loose from the rocks at low tide. The meat of the abalone, sliced and pounded into steaks and broiled, is very tasty. The Indians also made good use of the shiny abalone shell. From

it they chipped and ground ornaments, knives, and fishhooks.

Kwamut had brought several fishhooks with him. He tied one end of his fishing line to the side of the balsa and baited a second fishhook. The fish went for the bait and soon Kwamut had two large fish, strung on a short piece of fiber rope, struggling on the floor of the raft.

"I will help your mother broil these for the evening meal," Sister said to Kwamut.

"Grandfather wants to see you," Kwamut told Little Singer the following morning. "He understands the language of the song you sang last night."

Grandfather lived in a little hut at the edge of the village. He was old, and his relatives thought he would soon die. Since it was the custom among these Indians not only to burn their dead, but also to burn the dead person's possessions and house, they had built a separate hut for the old man at a safe distance from the village. When he died they could burn it without any danger of setting fire to the other houses in the village.

Little Singer had never before seen a man as old as Grandfather. After he entered the hut and his eyes had become used to the darkness, he kept staring at him. It was impolite to stare, but Little Singer could not help it. The old man was very thin and his skin, grown pale from living indoors, out of the sun, seemed to be stretched tightly over his bony frame. His long hair was completely white. His dark eyes, sunk in folds and wrinkles, looked back at the boy. He was old, and he had a right to look directly at anyone he wanted to look at. But Little Singer felt ashamed to have been caught staring. He lowered his eyes to the old man's bony brown chest, covered with necklaces, and then to his thin thighs and soft buckskin kilt.

"Grandfather," Kwamut said, "this is the boy who sang the song."

The old man spoke to Little Singer. "Truly you have been given a great gift, Grandson," he said. "I heard your song even as far as this house. It was good to hear a song again."

"We came to hear you talk, Grandfather," Kwamut said. "Little Singer does not under-

stand all of what we say. But he is a good lis-
tener." Kwamut brought out a little package of
tobacco and filled and lighted the old man's clay
pipe.

Grandfather pulled on the pipe a few times,
brushed his white hair back from his forehead,
and began. "This that I am going to tell you I
heard many times, but not from our own people.
This is told by a people who live far inland,
farther even than your village. Their lands are
beautiful, full of canyons and hills. They make
many things they trade with us. They call themselves Cahuilla, the Great People.

"I heard the stories I am going to tell you from
their old men when I went to trade shells with
them and became their friend and learned to
speak their language. My memory was good then,
and I have not forgotten anything I have heard,
old as I am. We will start at the beginning."

Little Singer spent many days listening to

Grandfather. Sometimes Grandfather felt tired and when Little Singer came to see him, he lay on his bed and would not even return the boy's greeting or thank him for the food he had brought. Little Singer would light the old man's pipe, sit by him for a while, and then return to the village. Quite often Sister came with Little Singer, as well as old friends of Grandfather's. They all listened carefully when the old man felt like telling legends. After a visit with him, Little Singer used to go over in his mind the things he had heard, repeating them over and over again to himself. In this way the legends became fixed in his mind, as they were fixed in the minds of the Cahuilla Indians, to whom they belonged.

The beliefs of the Indians of southern California came to them from their ancestors. From grandfather and grandmother, from father and mother to sons and daughters, these beliefs were told and retold. Time and time again, the boys and girls heard these tales (or myths, as we call them) at their evening firesides. Over and over again they heard them, till these myths became a part of their memory, a part they could never forget. When a man grew old, it was his turn to tell them to his grandchildren, as he had heard them in the words of his elders. Thus Little Singer listened to the myths and legends Grandfather told, and could retell them in the words Grandfather had used. These were sacred stories, and it was best to tell them just as he had heard them.

Like most of the legends Little Singer had heard, the Cahuilla stories began with the birth of the two boys—the two creators of the world—whom the Cahuilla called Mukat and Tamayoit. These legends always began with the words: "At first there was darkness. There was no earth, no sky. All was emptiness."

The two boys hatched out of two eggs and grew very fast. They were able to speak the moment they were born. And, like most brothers, they began to argue and compete and play tricks on each other. Each wanted to do things his own way.

The two brothers decided to drive away the darkness with tobacco smoke. But first they had to make tobacco. Both boys put their hands into their mouths, and brought out tobacco. Mukat brought out one kind, Tamayoit another kind—a tobacco of a lighter color. Now they needed pipes in which to smoke their tobacco. Again the brothers put their hands to their mouths, and this time brought forth clay. They made many pipes from the clay.

With a hot coal that Mukat took out of his mouth, he lighted his pipe. "Here is the pipe." Mukat offered it to Tamayoit, just as every man since then offers his pipe to a friend.

It was dark, and Tamayoit groped for the pipe. "I am holding it high," Mukat said. Actually he held it low. Tamayoit, always suspicious of Mukat's tricks, reached low for the pipe and got it. As Tamayoit got his pipe ready, he said to Mukat, "I'm holding it low." He really held it low.

Mukat expected his brother to play a trick on him, too. He reached high for the pipe, and of course missed it.

"You are not as wise as you think," Tamayoit teased Mukat.

As the darkness began to lift with the tobacco smoke, the boys could see well enough to begin creating the earth. After they made the earth they made the oceans to hold the earth. They made plants for both the land and the water, and all sorts of creatures to live on the land and in the water. They made the sky and put stars in it to make more light.

It was now time to make people.

Tamayoit made his people so fast that Mukat grew suspicious. He quickly created the sun so he could see exactly what Tamayoit was up to. The sun was too hot, and Mukat let it slip away and go up in the sky, where it has remained to this day. By the light of the sun, Mukat saw why Tamayoit had been able to work so fast. His people were alike on both sides. Each had two faces. Tamayoit had not bothered to separate their fingers and toes, so they had webbed fingers and toes.

"Your people don't look right," Mukat complained.

"They won't have to turn around to see behind them," Tamayoit explained. "And they won't drop things between their fingers."

But Mukat was very unhappy about the way Tamayoit's people looked. He started to argue. Tamayoit was tired of arguing with Mukat. He called together all the people he had made and took them underground, to another world. As Tamayoit and his people were settling underground, they pushed up the earth to make room for themselves. As they pushed, the earth cracked, making deep canyons. They pushed up parts of the earth, forming mountains and valleys. The sky became bent as it curved to make room for the rising mountains. The earth shook so that the water from the ocean ran into the cracks in the earth and made rivers and springs, lakes and waterfalls. That is why the earth looks as it does today.

5

THE TOLOACHE CEREMONY

The Indians of southern California called the boys' initiation ceremony the toloache (taw-law'-ah-chay) ceremony, because an important part of it was the drinking of toloache—a drink prepared from boiled Jimson weed. Kwamut's family had been preparing for the ceremony for a long time. The women had dried many fish and stored basketfuls of acorns for the feasts that were part of the ceremony. Kwamut was staying now with the three friends who were also going to be initiated. Every evening the old men of the village, who were in charge of the ceremony, talked to the boys, to prepare them for the event.

Because Little Singer had come especially for this ceremony, these men made him welcome. Unlike the younger boys, who lived in the village and were not yet considered old enough to learn the sacred details of the ceremony, Little Singer was allowed to enter the ceremonial rooms. He was free to go about to watch and learn.

The night the ceremony was to begin, Little Singer was ready long before a messenger knocked on the entrance to their compartment. He had bathed, and Mother had combed and greased his hair and given him one of her necklaces, so he would look especially nice for the occasion.

The ceremony started with drinking toloache.

The Jimson weed, or thorn apple, as it is also called, is a poisonous plant. Its large flowers are trumpet-shaped and range in color from white to violet. The fruit is prickly and, if eaten, would make people ill. But the Indians discovered that a drink could be prepared from the crushed root of the Jimson weed, mixed with water. This drink was not poisonous if only a spoonful of it was swallowed. More of this drink could have been deadly, but this small amount only had the power to make the drinker dizzy at first and then unconscious for a while. It also brought him dreams. Every Indian regarded dreams as something special, caused by the spirits, so each boy looked forward to a dream during the toloache ceremony. The Indians believed the Jimson weed was very strong medicine, and each boy had to drink it once in his lifetime, as part of his initiation into manhood.

The toloache ceremony, which always started at night, was held in a special house outside the village. It had an extra room that was very dark, where the boys could rest and dream after taking the drink. A shaman prepared the toloache with great care, using only special ceremonial bowls, which were kept in the chief's house, to boil it.

Kwamut and the three other boys lined up in single file outside the house. Each boy had an older male relative to guide him and watch over him. Little Singer saw Kwamut enter the house and kneel down before the carved soapstone bowl that held the drink. His uncle put a restraining hand on Kwamut's forehead, to make sure the boy did not take too much toloache. The other relatives did the same thing with their charges.

After taking the drink, the boys filed out, again in single line, and began to circle around the fire. Everyone in the village had come to watch the ceremony. Little Singer sat near the fire with several other singers. They took turns in singing their songs. Soon Kwamut and the other boys began to feel dizzy. Confused by what was happening to him, Kwamut rubbed his eyes and forehead and shook his head, trying to shake off his dizziness. But his uncle put his arms about Kwamut, carried him away from the fire, and laid him on the floor in the dark room, where Kwamut instantly fell asleep.

Later Kwamut told Little Singer what he had

undergone. He said he must have slept soundly the first day without dreaming. On the second day he began to awaken, but was not sure whether he was actually experiencing things, or dreaming them. He dreamed he was going fishing in a boat with several men. Suddenly his spear and fishing tackle slipped overboard. Kwamut dived into the sea to recover his gear. After he had got hold of it and was about to get back into the boat, he found that the boat had gone on without him. He saw the men kneeling in the boat, dipping their double paddles rhythmically—first left, then right, then left again. He tried to call to them, but no sound would come out of his mouth. Kwamut watched the men and the boat getting smaller and smaller in the distance, till the men's heads were no bigger than acorns and the boat was the size of a child's toy.

Kwamut began to swim for shore, but he felt very tired and could hardly move his legs and arms. Suddenly something pushed itself under him. It was a tiny fish, the size of his finger. The fingerling took Kwamut's fishhook into its mouth and swam ahead, pulling Kwamut along. They were within sight of shore, when a big shark came

charging down upon them. Its mouth open and full of teeth, the shark swallowed the little fish and Kwamut's hook and spear. It was about to attack Kwamut when a wave lifted the boy high up and threw him ashore. He felt himself striking against the rocks so hard that he awoke.

It took Kwamut a while to realize just where he was. He lay thinking of his dream, wondering about its meaning. He knew, of course, that never again must he eat the kind of fish that had saved his life. If ever he caught one, he must let it go back into the ocean. It would be his helper throughout his life.

Outside, Kwamut heard the men singing and the heel-and-toe stamping of the ceremonial dance. Next he heard Little Singer's voice. It made Kwamut happy to hear it. He tried to get up, but felt too dizzy. He noticed that two of the boys who were being initiated with him were still sleeping. Seeing Kwamut move, his uncle brought him a bowl of warm water to drink. Kwamut drank the water and fell asleep again. He slept through that entire day and night.

When he next awoke, Kwamut was hungry. His uncle gave him some hot acorn mush to sip. The other boys were also eating hot mush. Four days and nights had passed since they had drunk the toloache.

Kwamut was now ready to get up. His uncle

tied a fiber belt tightly around his waist, so he would not feel the pangs of hunger. The boys were to eat very little during the first month after their initiation and were not to touch meat for several months. If the boys ate meat before they were supposed to, it was believed that they would never be successful hunters.

In addition to the singing, there were nightly dances and special performances. The California Indians looked upon these performances as a show of special magic powers. One very colorful dance was the feather dance. Men wearing tall head-dresses made of feathers of many colors danced around and around the fire. Suddenly the sound of rattles and the dancing stopped. The men tore their headdresses off and brushed them into the fire—in and out. The wonder of it was that neither the headdresses nor the dancers' hands were in the least singed by the flames.

Even more impressive were the fire-eaters. On the eighth night of the ceremony a fire-eater stepped forward and sang a song he had learned in a dream. Then he took a live coal from the fire and put it into his mouth. Everyone in the audience saw the man's entire face glow red from the hot coal inside his mouth. There were two such fire-eaters in the village. To please the people and the spirits, they always performed this magic act at the village's ceremonies.

Little Singer noticed many strange faces in the crowd that had gathered to listen to the songs and watch the dances and the magic. These people had come from other villages. They, too, had walked for several days in order to attend the ceremony. To attend a ceremony, everyone believed, was to share its good effects. The benefits expected—good health, good luck in hunting, and a long life—would be theirs too, because they had been present. In addition, these strangers were invited to take part by singing their songs. Little Singer liked to listen to a song several times before he tried to sing it. He found that his memory continued to serve him well. During Kwamut's toloache ceremony, Little Singer learned several new songs and sang them nightly.

During the day the boys who were being initiated rested and slept. They were getting very thin. Kwamut told Little Singer that he was hungry all the time, no matter how much he tightened his belt. He could hardly wait for the ceremony to be over.

At last the four boys were called to the dance ground. There, inside a trench, the men shaped a figure made of grass. Along the effigy's body lay four stones. Kwamut jumped from the edge of the trench onto the first stone. With the help of his uncle he skipped from stone to stone and then jumped out of the trench. This meant that he would enjoy a long life. If Kwamut had stumbled or slipped, it would have meant that he would die young.

The final step was the sand-painting ceremony. The sand painting looked like the one in the girls' ceremony. There were the same black border and the same symbols inside the circle. Each boy bent over the sand painting while the chief spoke to him. "See the lines," he said. "This is bear-mountain-lion. These lines are living things. They are going to catch you if you are not good and do not respect your elders. These lines are going to kill you if you do not believe in them. If you do believe, everybody is going to see your goodness and you will kill bear-mountain-lion. You will be famous, and you will be praised

by everyone. Your name will be heard everywhere.

"And this—this is the raven. He will kill

you with his bow and arrow if you do not offer
people the game you shoot. You must always eat
sparingly. Do not eat at night the food that has
been left for the morning meal. You must never
be angry with your relatives. The earth hears

you. The sky, the woods, and the mountains see you. If you believe this you will live to grow old. You will see your sons and daughters grow up. You will give them good counsel, as we are doing now, when you get older. If, when hunting, you should kill a rabbit or deer and an old man should ask you for it, hand it to him at once! Do not be angry when you give it to him. He will praise you, and you will kill many more animals. You will be able to shoot straight with your bow.

"When you die, your spirit will rise to the sky and people will blow three times to help your spirit rise. Everywhere it will be heard that you have died. And everyone will be sad because you have gone.

"This is how our people have always counseled their sons and daughters. In this manner you will give counsel to your sons and daughters.

"When you die you will be seen as a star in the sky. And you will live there forever."

Kwamut, kneeling beside the sand painting,

took into his mouth the small ball of sage meal and salt that was offered to him and spat it into the center of the painting, where a small hole had been dug. His uncle swept up the painting. He carried the sand out and hid it in a sacred place so that no one should ever walk on it. This ended the toloache ceremony.

Little Singer and his family were ready to leave. It would be his parents' turn now to accumulate food and small things for gifts, and make arrangements for Little Singer's initiation ceremony the following year.

Again Mother and Sister packed their belongings into their two large pack baskets. Mother talked as she worked, saying how much they had enjoyed their stay in this village. The people had been very kind to them. They liked the fresh fish, the abalone, and the other shellfish they had eaten daily.

Little Singer wondered why Kwamut, who had

become their best friend, had not been in to see them. Perhaps he was away hunting. Certainly he was nowhere in the village.

The women put on their basket caps. Little Singer and Father were helping them put the heavy baskets into their carrying nets, when the chief and one of his wives, Kwamut's mother, entered their compartment. As a gift, Kwamut's mother carried a beautiful carved soapstone bowl inlaid with abalone shell. Sister quickly dropped her basket and slipped out of the compartment. After Mother had recovered from her surprise at this handsome gift, she asked the visitors to sit down.

The chief spoke. "My son has asked us to speak for him about your daughter. We have watched her during your stay with us, and we think she is a fine worker and will make a good wife for our son. We are of the Coyote people and we know you are of the Wildcat people. It is permitted for our people to marry your people.

Our son is still young. May we come in a year to your village? Our son will then marry your daughter and take her back to live here, as is our custom."

Mother and Father looked at each other. They knew Sister liked Kwamut. They liked him too. Judging from Sister's behavior, she knew that Kwamut had intended to ask permission to marry her. Mother took the bowl from Kwamut's mother. This was the same as a spoken promise that Sister would wait for Kwamut.

Kwamut joined them on the outskirts of his village and walked for a while beside Sister. Father and Mother went on ahead with the chief and Kwamut's mother and let the young people talk by themselves. Sister had always been shy. Little Singer tried to remember if he had ever before seen her talk with Kwamut alone, but he could not recall a single instance. Some things escape me, Little Singer thought to himself. I must watch more carefully.

As Little Singer turned for a last look at the Great Water and Kwamut's village, he was surprised to see columns of dust rising from a hill at one side of the village. Soon bearded men, riding large animals—larger than dogs—and wearing shiny shirts and helmets appeared at the top of the hill. Little Singer remembered the stories he had heard from inland Indians who had seen Spaniards before. "Palefaces!" he cried, unable to believe his eyes.

The palefaces stopped at the top of the hill and began to put up a large wooden cross. The Indian party stood a long time, watching them. "We must go back to our people," the chief said.

"We will go back with you," Little Singer's father said. "You may need our help."

6

MISSION DAYS

The southern Californians had lived as hunters and food gatherers for many centuries. Their way of life might have remained the same, or changed very little, for many more centuries had it not been for the ambitions of white explorers. The search for a short cut to speed ships from one ocean to another had continued long after Columbus discovered America. Spain founded a large empire in Mexico, then called New Spain. Her merchant ships, loaded with hides, tallow, cocoa, gold, and silver from her colonies, sailed east and west.

Westward lay the Orient, with its silks and spices. The Spanish ships returning from Asian ports had to round the Cape of Good Hope to bring their cargo across the Atlantic to Spain and other European markets. This was too long a journey. The merchant ships were badly equipped. The sailors were always ailing; many died. If only a waterway across North America could be found, joining the two oceans!

Although much of the American continent had been explored by 1750, southern California was still an unknown land. Spanish explorers, sailing up the Pacific coast from New Spain searched for a waterway—an opening similar to our Panama Canal. Every inlet and bay along the California coast held out the hope that it might cut across the continent. Eagerly the Spanish explorers went up the bays, only to find their way barred by land. One such explorer, Juan Rodrigues Cabrillo found a bay in 1542 and sailed hopefully up it. When land appeared at the water's end, he named it the Bay of Cabrillo.

The curious, wary coastal Indians watched the men step ashore and plant a large wooden cross to claim this land for the Spanish crown. The Indians did not know the meaning of the cross. After the white men with the dark beards had left, the cross became weather-beaten, and the Indians took it down and burned it for firewood.

Some of the Indians told the palefaces, in sign language, that they had heard stories, while trading with inland Indians, that other parties of palefaces had been seen to the east of them. They gave Cabrillo and his men fresh water to drink, dried berries, and acorn bread, and were happy to receive in return the pieces of red cloth, the beads, and the other trinkets the Spaniard gave them.

Sebastián Vizcaíno followed Cabrillo in 1602. He was not sure that the bay he explored was the same one that Cabrillo had discovered. He called it the Bay of San Diego—its name today.

Of course neither Vizcaíno nor the others who followed him found a waterway that would link the Atlantic and Pacific Oceans, but they claimed these new lands for the Spanish Crown. The Spanish government in New Spain was always looking for new regions to develop and the

Church was looking for more converts to Christianity. Franciscan friars were busy building missions and cathedrals in New Spain and converting the Indians there. They wanted to do the same for the Indians of California.

In 1769 Father Junípero Serra left New Spain to travel overland to these unexplored lands, where he planned to start missions. With him went soldiers and Spanish settlers, cattle, horses, and sheep, oxen and wagons. Boats with more supplies were to meet Father Serra in San Diego Bay.

It was Father Serra's men whom Little Singer had seen at the crest of the hill near Kwamut's village. He and his family returned to the chief's village, and throughout the day the Indians watched the palefaces, who were putting up shelters for themselves.

The Spaniards did not speak to the Indians, and the Indians did not approach them. Although

the palefaces were settling on land that belonged
to the village, they did not ask the village chief's

permission to use it. They found the spring near
the village and milled around it, drinking, washing themselves, and watering their animals.

Toward evening the strangers' limping, gray-robed chief entered the Indian village, and Kwamut's father met him. The old paleface pointed to himself. "Padre Serra (Father Serra)," he said, over and over again. It was clear that he was not afraid to have the Indians know his name. It was hard for the Indians to pronounce the rolling *R* in the strange speech, however. They had already nicknamed the padre the Limping One. They themselves, of course, did not mention either their names or nicknames.

Little Singer went up close to the old paleface and watched his mouth as he talked. "Padre Serra, Serra," Little Singer repeated after him. Puzzled, the old paleface looked down at the boy intently. He put his hand on Little Singer's shoulder. *"Hablas Español?"* he asked. ("Do you speak Spanish?") Little Singer, eager to learn the new language, repeated the padre's words, trying to imitate his voice. *"Hablas Español? Hablas Español?"* He was happy to have learned four words in the strange speech.

It was not only the language of the Spaniards that was strange to the Indians. Their ways were equally strange. At sunset, the huge bell which Father Serra had hung in one of the oak trees pealed forth. All the Spanish people gathered around it. Father Serra donned a red and gold robe with a white lace collar, and his men knelt while he began to speak and make gestures. The Indians knew that this was a ceremony and they stood respectfully silent, watching. They were amazed that instead of dancing, as they would have done, the strangers remained in one place, kneeling, with bowed heads.

Father Serra asked the Indians to kneel, too, and they did. They were afraid of the large, shiny cross he carried before him. Their own prayer sticks were sacred and held great power. This cross might hold power too. It would do them no harm, they thought, if they knelt like the palefaces. They even promised to come to the ceremony the following day, since the white man's spirits seemed to wish it. The Indians did not want to offend the white man's spirits, any more than they wanted to offend their own spirits.

The Spaniards immediately set to work, preparing to build the mission of San Diego. A few days later a boat loaded with supplies for Father Serra entered the harbor.

In the meantime, the Indian women worked about their households as usual, grinding acorns, baking bread, and weaving their baskets. The men hunted, but they did not go too far from their villages, because the white men, with their strange weapons, were walking through the woods, also looking for game. Little Singer and his family remained in Kwamut's village, and Sister was married to Kwamut. They built two huts next to the chief's house—one for the young couple, the other for Little Singer's family.

One morning Kwamut and a few men from his village were watching the Spaniards chop down trees. The sharp metal axes and saws of the pale-faces felled the trees quickly, one after another. In one afternoon, the Bearded Ones did an amount of work that would have taken the Indians, with their wedges, a month to do. Those tools were, indeed, remarkable.

One of the Spaniards handed his ax to Kwamut. Kwamut had watched him closely. He picked up the ax and swung it at a tree as the Bearded One had done. The ax made a deep cut in the wood. Having tried it, Kwamut wanted to return the ax to its owner, but the gray-robed man stopped him. He put the ax back into Kwamut's hands and ordered him to continue. The same thing happened to several other Indians. They had merely wanted to try the new tools. Now they found themselves working for the palefaces.

The Indians were forced to work till late in the afternoon. They were used to hard work, but they liked to stop when they began to feel tired. The Bearded Ones would not let them stop. Finally one man, Kwamut's uncle, let the ax slip out of his hands and dropped to the ground with fatigue. In an instant, a Spaniard swung his leather whip over Uncle's head. He would have struck him, but Kwamut, with the agility of a hunter, covered Uncle's body with his own. The whip descended on Kwamut again and again, leaving bloody welts.

Kwamut was angry, but he had never fought another man and he saw that his own people were outnumbered. He picked up Uncle and carried him home, on his bleeding back, to their village.

Sister had a similar experience that afternoon while she was gathering wood and seeds with her two young sisters-in-law. A white man was building a fire in Father Serra's camp. He hung a huge pot over it. The women, who had never seen such a large pot, stopped to admire it. The man asked them to come nearer, and gave them some beads and thread. Then he pointed to the pot, inviting them in sign language to cook the meat he was cutting up. The Indian girls helped him. In their village men did not do any cooking. They were glad to help this white man who did not have a woman to take care of him.

That night, the men of the village held a counsel and decided to abandon their village and move farther south, away from the palefaces. Little Singer's father invited them to join his village, but the men wanted to stay close to the ocean, because they depended on fish and shellfish for food. They decided to leave the following night. In order not to arouse suspicion, the women helped the white man cook his meals the next day and came home late that afternoon. Everyone was packed and ready to go. After dark they slipped out of the village, one by one. The next day, when the Spanish soldiers came to call the men and women to work, the village was deserted. In their anger at having been outwitted, the soldiers set fire to the huts. In a short time, Kwamut's village was a pile of ashes.

The Indians had been on the trail for two days when the soldiers caught them, whipped the chief, and forced the people to turn back. They did not even give them time to rebuild their homes. Men, women, and children were herded into temporary shelters at the building site of the Mission of San Diego, and put to work. Although the Indians did not know it, they were never again to live their old way of life. From this time on, in spite of many Indian uprisings, they were forced to work for their Spanish masters, and were called Mission Indians.

The building of the Mission of San Diego took about a year. Father Serra wanted it built of adobe, or clay bricks, which he ordered the Indians—now called the Diegueño—to make. The Diegueño had not made adobe brick before, although other Indians in North America knew about adobe. It was easy to learn to make it. For many days, the Indians carried clay to a flat field, where the men pounded and kneaded it till it was smooth. When it was ready, the men and women carried water in their large basket jars, or ollas, and poured it over the clay. Again the clay was kneaded and worked with hands and feet until it

was evenly mixed. Then dry grass was added to the mixture and it was mixed some more. Finally, the adobe was ready to be poured into forms— wooden squares twelve inches long and four inches deep. When the adobe mixture in the forms was dry and hard, the Indians removed the forms and the bricks were left to dry thoroughly in the sun. After they had turned each brick over to dry the bottom, they stacked them, ready for use.

The walls of the mission were laid by piling adobe bricks one on top of another and cementing them with mud. Next a coat of mud plaster was smeared over the walls. After the plaster dried, the walls were painted white with white clay. The first roof of the mission was made of thatch, but this proved to be a fire hazard. A year later the Mission of San Diego was set afire in an Indian uprising and burned down. The Diegueño had to rebuild it with a roof made of tile.

The Indians soon became very skillful at making tiles. The women prepared fine clay for the tiles in much the same way as they used to prepare clay for pottery making. After the clay had been mixed with water, the men shaped it into squares of an even thickness, which they patted over logs to dry. The rounded tiles were then fired, or baked. The firing, too, was like the firing of pottery. The tiles were spread out on the ground so they did not touch, and a hot fire was built around them. When the firing was finished, the tiles were a deep red color. Later, the Spanish taught the Diegueño to build ovens, or kilns, for firing tiles.

All the missions were built like forts, with thick walls, small openings for windows, and heavy doors. Each mission had one or two bell towers. High walls enclosed the building, and the only entrance was through a gate that opened from the inside. A person could enter the mission only if the people inside wanted to let him in. The whole mission was about the size of one of our square city blocks.

The buildings of the mission formed another square inside the high walls. All these buildings, including a church and its cemetery, the friars' living quarters, the storerooms, and the workshops, faced an open space in the center, called the patio. Some missions also had dormitories for unmarried Indians: one for the men on one side of the patio, and one for the women on the other side. Married couples and their children lived in huts, which were built outside the mission walls.

Each mission tried to be as self-supporting as possible. After having the fields plowed, the Spanish planted corn, wheat, melons, and potatoes. They also planted young fruit trees which they had brought with them. With continuous watering and care, orchards of pear trees, plums, peaches, and apricots began to thrive. Grapes also grew well.

The Indians were not used to the continuous labor and care the fields and orchards demanded. The friars forced them to carry water, hoe the fields, and tend the orchards. Everyone had to work, even the children, and the work never stopped. There was no longer time for the Indians to get together, or to attend the ceremonies that were so important to them.

The food prepared at the mission kitchens was not to the Diegueño's liking. They had never eaten a great deal, but they had had many feasts, which made up for the lack of plentiful daily food. At the missions they were fed the same diet—stew, or mush, and a slice or two of bread— day after day. They were given very little meat or fish. The women had no time to go out to gather berries, plants, and acorns as they used to do.

Wheat bread, which was unknown to the southern Californians before the coming of the Spanish, took the place of acorn bread. The friars taught the Diegueño women how to bake it in the little beehive ovens the men built for them. The women prepared the dough for the bread the night before they planned to bake, and let it rise overnight. The next day, they built a small fire inside the oven to heat it. When the fire burned down, they swept the oven clean, kneaded the dough again, and shaped it into small loaves. They placed the loaves on a long-handled paddle and slid them into the heated oven to bake.

When an Indian was sick in his own village, his relatives and the chief had taken charge and asked shamans to cure him. At the mission, he did not receive all this attention. The friars merely used simple remedies, in which the Indians had no faith. As soon as an Indian was well enough to get up, he had to start working again.

Some of the Indians became very good sheepherders. They liked moving from pasture to pasture with the sheep. Their families went with them, and the women gathered seeds and acorns. They lived in shelters and cared for their children as they had done in their own villages. Twice a year, the sheep were rounded up and driven to the mission to be counted and sheared.

The Indian women already knew how to spin. Now the padres taught them to weave cloth.

They learned to comb and card wool and spin it into yarn. They also learned how to dye the yarn and weave it into cloth on looms built with the help of the Spanish carpenters. Soon all the padres' clothing and the kilts, skirts, and blouses worn by the Indian men and women were made on the mission's looms.

Before the coming of the Spanish, the Diegueño had never seen horses, because there weren't any in the Americas. The men and boys soon learned

to care for horses, as well as for mules, oxen, and burros. They liked the horses, because they were such handsome animals. The Indians were good riders, but the padres forbade them to ride horses. No Indian was allowed to own a horse.

The Indians also learned blacksmithing. Horses had to be shod and horseshoes made for them. They learned to make all sorts of metal tools—hoes, axes, saws, and files—and to forge wrought iron. With iron punches and steel knives, they began to tool leather. Saddles made of tooled leather, inlaid with silver, soon became the pride of the Spanish settlers.

For many centuries the Indian women had tanned buckskin. They now began to tan the hides of horses and cattle, one of the missions' main items of trade with the merchant ships that stopped in the Bay of San Diego. They soaked the hide in lime water to loosen the hair. Then they patiently scraped the hair and flesh from the hide, using metal-edged scrapers that were more efficient than the old bone scrapers they had once used. When all the hair was removed, they rubbed the hide with an oily mixture made from animals' brains, scraped off some of the oil, and stretched the hide by pegging it into the ground. When it had dried, it was folded and stacked in the storerooms to await the arrival of a merchant ship.

The meat from cattle was dried and stored too.

The fat was melted in large kettles. When it cooled and hardened, it was packed in boxes. This fat, or tallow, was an important article of trade.

Some of the tallow was mixed with beeswax, produced by the bees the padres had brought with them, and made into candles. The Indians melted the tallow and wax in a large kettle. Wicks for the candles dangled from a large wheel hanging over the kettle. As the wheel turned, the wicks were dipped into the kettle again and again. Gradually the tallow coated the wicks, shaping a long candle.

The blaze of candles in the church during religious festivals, or *fiestas*, delighted the Indians. When a *fiesta* was about to begin, it was always announced by the pealing of the bells in the church tower. The Indians from the surrounding villages came to see the sight—as beautiful as the stars in the sky. Those among them who had been baptized entered the church and knelt on the floor while the padre, in his red and gold robes, conducted the service. Sometimes Indians permitted themselves to be baptized so they could watch the service from the inside.

Little Singer was one of the first Indian boys to learn the Christian ritual and music well enough to become a choirboy. He had learned Spanish quickly. When Kwamut's people were being herded back to their burned-down village, he had stayed near the soldiers so he could listen to them talk. He repeated Spanish words to himself, trying to get used to the sound of the strange language. He pointed to trees, rocks, animals, and birds on the trail and memorized the Spanish words for them that the soldiers taught him. At the end of the two-days' march, Little Singer knew more than two dozen words in Spanish. As time went on, he asked the small choirboys to sing the songs they were learning, and learned them himself.

Surely this young Indian must have been baptized somewhere, the padres thought when they heard Little Singer chant with the choir. They invited him to their quarters for long talks. Little Singer always listened carefully. At the end of each talk, he knew a few more words in Spanish. By the time the Mission of San Diego was completed, he knew Spanish quite well. Few of the padres learned to speak the Indian languages and dialects well. After a while, Little Singer worked at his loom only a few hours a day; the rest of the time the padres ordered him to go with them as an interpreter. He was forced to live in the men's barracks at the mission, where he would be on hand when the padres wanted him.

Little Singer was never baptized, however, and his people trusted him. Soon he became their chief and spokesman. Working for his people kept Little Singer very busy. There was a great deal of sickness and suffering among the Indians. In those days overseers were severe; they punished not only the Indians who worked for them, but their own men, too, if they did anything wrong.

There was never a day that someone was not flogged or jailed for a misdemeanor. Some Indian offenders were shot.

Many more Indians died from disease. Spanish soldiers and settlers brought with them the germs of diseases unknown to the Indians. Their bodies had built up no resistance to them. From the time the mission of San Diego was built until it was closed in 1833, the Indians' death rate was twice as high as their birth rate.

The Indians who lived at the missions were the chief victims of disease. The mission houses and dormitories were crowded and dirty; disease spread rapidly. The Indians who had escaped into the hills fared better, but soldiers were after them all the time to come to the missions to work.

Kwamut's father died during a measles epidemic that wiped out his village and emptied the dormitories. He had attended church a few times, and the friars would not permit his body to be burned. This was the Indian custom, but it was forbidden by the friars' religion. He was buried in a coffin made for him by the carpenters.

Kwamut appealed to Little Singer and his relatives for help. One night men from a nearby village unearthed the body, carried it away, and burned it. They carefully filled the space with stones and covered it with earth, so the friars would not become suspicious.

A year later, the friars at the San Diego mission announced a *fiesta*. Kwamut and his family attended it. The friars thought the Indians were celebrating with them, but they were really singing mourning songs for their chief. Earlier, Kwamut had built an effigy of grass and burned it to honor his father. After his choir singing, Little Singer joined the Indians and sang for the mourning ceremony, which they believed would make the old chief's spirit regard them in peace and contentment, and watch over the few of them that were left.

Kwamut would have liked to follow the

mourning ceremony with a feast, but neither he nor Sister could get extra food from the mission kitchens. They were unable to get food anywhere else. The fields, orchards, and gardens of the mission covered their old food-gathering territories. If they were caught gathering seeds or acorns there, they would be flogged for trespassing.

The Mission of San Diego was the first mission in southern California, but soon others were built. Not all of them were made of adobe; some were built with the yellow stone that the Spanish found in abundance in the hills. Some took a year or two to build; others took as long as ten years. In a little more than fifty years, twenty-one missions were erected along the southern California coast. Each one was within a day's journey of its neighbor, so the Spaniards could easily keep in touch with each other and help each other.

Like the Diegueño, other Indian groups who

lived near the missions were forced to give up their way of life and work for the Spanish. The people were herded into dormitories or huts outside the mission walls, and made to work in the fields and orchards. Many of them also died of diseases caught from their masters.

Here is a list of all the missions, with the dates when building began and the names of the Indian groups who helped to build them:

1. 1769   San Diego de Alcalá (Diegueño)
2. 1770   San Carlos Borromeo
3. 1771   San Antonio de Padua
4. 1771   San Gabriel Arcangel (Serrano and Gabrielino)
5. 1772   San Luis Obispo de Tolosa (Chumash)
6. 1776   San Francisco de Asís
7. 1776   San Juan Capistrano (Juaneño)
8. 1777   Santa Clara de Asís
9. 1782   San Buenaventura (Chumash)

10. 1786 Santa Barbara (Chumash)
11. 1787 La Purisima Concepcion (Chumash)
12. 1791 Santa Cruz
13. 1791 Nuestra Señora de la Soledad
14. 1797 San José de Guadalupe
15. 1797 San Juan Bautista
16. 1797 San Miguel Arcangel
17. 1797 San Fernando Rey de España
18. 1798 San Luis Rey de Francia (Luiseño)
19. 1804 Santa Ines (Chumash)
20. 1817 San Rafael Arcangel
21. 1823 San Francisco Solano

7

THE END OF THE TRAIL

Little Singer was nearing the end of his trail.
He had lived a hundred years—a whole century.
He was now living in a little hut, some distance
from his people's village. The women of the village built the hut for him, as was the custom. A
young girl from the village came to see him every

few days. She brought him a little food and combed his long white hair. Once she asked him to look at himself in the mirror she had brought with her. Little Singer was surprised to see how old he really looked—as old, pale, and white-haired as the storyteller in Kwamut's village long ago. He still remembered the Cahuilla stories the old man had told him. He liked to tell them to the children who came to see him.

The Cahuilla Indians, who lived too far from the missions to be drafted for work, were better off than the other Indian groups and there were more of them left even now. They were now under the control of the United States government. Young Cahuilla men sometimes came to hear Little Singer's tales too. They left him small gifts to show how grateful they were that he, a Luiseño Indian, told their legends so carefully.

Little Singer's voice had lost much of its former resonance. At times it cracked, and he ran out of breath. But his people—the few that remained—

always asked him to sing when they visited him. So he was still able to please others, and his old age had not yet become a burden to himself or to any of his people. He wished he had a grand-child to care for him, but he had never married. When he was a young man at the mission of San Diego and later at the mission of San Luis Rey—among his own people—he had been kept too busy translating for the padres, and helping his people, to think about himself and about raising a family.

He kept hoping, like all the Mission Indians, that they would one day revolt and chase the pa-dres and settlers from their lands. But the up-risings that flared up were quickly subdued by the Spanish soldiers, with much suffering, punish-ment, and loss of life for the Indians.

Little Singer was in his late seventies when there was another great change in the lives of his people. In 1821 the Mexicans revolted from Spain and set up a republic. In 1833 the Mexican government ordered the missions to be closed and the mission lands to be divided among the Mission Indians. Turmoil and land grabbing followed this decree. Spanish settlers and landowners seized most of the mission lands and left only the most barren tracts for the Indians. Mexicans kept crossing the border, carrying papers to show that their new government had made them gifts of land in upper California. The Mission Indians on these lands were ordered to move. There was no one to speak for them.

The Luiseño moved farther inland. They tried to do a little farming and sheepherding on the barren lands where they now had to live, but they had no money for seeds or tools. Most of them were half-starved between the meager harvests of acorns and grass seed. Some went to work for the Mexican landlords and again sank into the same kind of slavery or peonage they had endured during the mission days.

In 1846, during the Mexican War, the United

States took over upper California. Little Singer had just turned ninety when the news of the new government reached his village. Yankees, or *Anglos*, as the Spanish called them, swarmed in from the East. These white men did not want Indians living in California at all. The Diegueño were driven at gun point from their old fishing grounds and acorn groves. If a group of *Anglos* suspected that a Luiseño had stolen some of their horses, they did not even stop to talk the matter over with the village chiefs. Firing their guns, they came and set fire to the village. The villagers, exhausted by persecution, did not even try to run away. They preferred to die in their own huts. Neighbors always brought Little Singer to sing for the dead. He sang all the mourning songs he knew, sure that the spirits of these Luiseño had at last found happiness and peace.

Although the land on which Little Singer and his people now lived had belonged to them for many centuries, they lived in constant fear of los-ing it. At any moment a party of *Anglos*, coming over the mountains in their covered wagons, might take a liking to the village's site and decide to settle there. With loud voices, they would order the Indians to get off the land and stay off. There was no way for the Indians to get justice. This had happened so many times before that Little Singer knew it would happen again. His people hid the trail to the spring. The women went for water only at dusk, so no white prowler would find their spring. Since water was so precious in that dry country, it could only mean trouble to let an outsider know where it was.

There were hardly any young men left in the village. They went away to look for work in the towns and ranches that were mushrooming all around them. Most of these young people no longer returned to the village. After their folks died, there was no one to return to.

Little Singer felt, without regret, that his end was coming soon. If only there were someone to whom he could teach the songs he knew, so they would not be lost! The white men had their songs written in books. He had seen these books at the missions. He wished he had learned to read and write, so he could write down his songs. Without them, the ceremonies of his people would have no power—no effect. It will be the end of my people, he thought, as he closed his eyes in weariness. . . .

Of the 30,000 Indians who once peopled southern California, less than 3000 remain today. None of the Chumash, the Gabrielino, the Luiseño, or the Juaneño Indians are left. There are still some scattered remnants of the Diegueño and Cahuilla. Most of the Indians in southern California today are newcomers, like their white neighbors. Like them, these Indians came from the East and the North in search of work in the citrus groves, the vineyards, and the ranches that now cover the former lands of the Indians of southern California. In 1870 the United States government began to buy lands in California for Indian reservations, in response to the public demand that something be done to better the

conditions of the Indians. Today there are twenty-eight such reservations in southern California. There are small gardens, orchards, and some cattle on these reservations. To many of the Indians these reservations are home, even though they have to leave them from time to time in search of work. Some like to return home, after the work is finished, to be with their own people. Others have lived all their lives with white neighbors. Their children have gone to school with white children. They have found work in the towns in which they live. These are home to them now.

Index

* Indicates illustrations.

139